PRIVATE LESSONS

M000230083

THE GUITAR LICK·TIONARY

BY DAVE HILL

ISBN 0-634-01471-4

HAL·LEONARD® CORPORATION

7777 W. BLUEMOUND RD. P.O. BOX 13819 MILWAUKEE, WI 53213

Visit Hal Leonard Online at
www.halleonard.com

INTRODUCTION

Music is a language, and each language has its own vocabulary. Whether you're speaking Spanish, French, German, or playing blues, rock, country, or jazz, the richer your vocabulary, the more creative you can be in expressing your thoughts and ideas. This book is a tool to help you expand your music vocabulary and provide some insight into the vast variety of phrases *(licks)* that make up different styles.

Of course, learning vocabulary alone doesn't teach you the grammar of a language. The skill of developing and connecting phrases in a spontaneous and inspired way requires a study of the music. No "one-stop shopping lick book" can substitute for a lot of listening, a lot of transcribing, and a lot of playing. This book, however, can be a great resource, opening your ears to the stylistic tricks and techniques that can sometimes be elusive.

The Guitar Licktionary will expand your appreciation of music and styles while inspiring new ideas that will ultimately become your own unique language. Good luck, and enjoy the journey!

HOW TO USE THIS BOOK

Each lick is described and notated alphabetically, and recorded on the accompanying CD, so you can hear and understand the concepts behind it. Throughout this book, the numbers in the audio symbols (◆) indicate the track where each lick will be found on the CD. (Because of audio constraints, most licks are doubled up—two to a track.) You can go through them all, find specific licks alphabetically, or use the index to find licks in a specific style.

TABLE OF CONTENTS

INDEX OF LICKS BY STYLE

A

① A • cid Jazz

This line adds color to a dominant chord. It starts off with an obvious C major triad, then implies a D major triad.

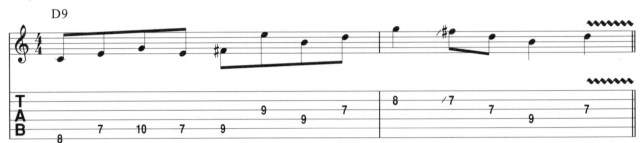

① Al • tered
(Cont'd)

This lick uses notes from the E altered scale and combines it with chromatic notes for an interesting sequence.

② Al • tered Se • quence

This V-to-I lick makes use of the diminished scale. It's a sequence that climbs up the neck on the top two strings. Try to make it as legato as possible. It could also be played on the second and third strings.

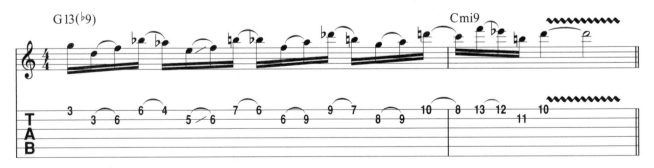

Al • tered Tri • ads

(Cont'd) This lick combines B♭ and G triads with notes from the diminished scale for an extended altered-dominant sound.

Al • tered Trick

Here's a trick you can play with your pentatonic blues licks: instead of playing major pentatonic off the root of the chord, play it off the ♭9 (up a half step from the root). This makes that basic blues lick sound like a sophisticated altered dominant sound. Compare the notes and you end up with a ♭9, ♯9, 11, ♯5, and ♭7.

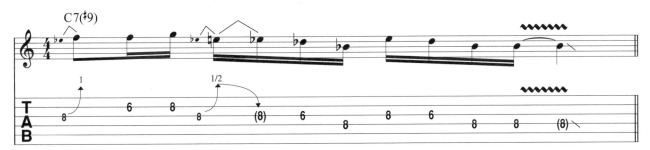

A • scend • ing Ly • di • an

(Cont'd) This is a neat idea that connects the patterns of G major with smooth shifts. Although it works well as a Lydian phrase, experiment with other chords in the key of G. Try Ami7 and D7.

B

4 **Bach Rock**

Here's a little tip of the hat to the classical rock players who owe so much to the great J.S. Bach. This fingering involves the entire neck and does so with efficient use of the left hand. Start slow with this one and gradually work up the tempo.

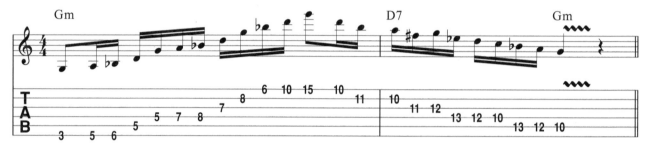

4 **B.B. • ish**

(Cont'd) Here's one from the blues master himself. Although you could play this lick in one position, it sounds better when kept on the top three strings. Make sure you slide off the G octaves at the end. Think of this lick as starting on the fifth measure of a shuffle blues in G.

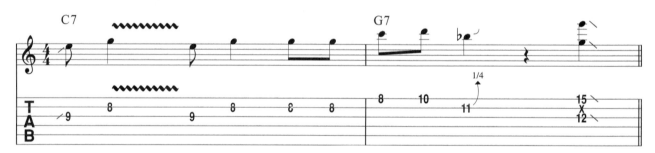

5 **Be • bop**

This Bebop line is great on the last six measures of a jazz blues. The chord tones are well placed on the downbeats, lending a clear outline to the changes. The lick finishes off with a bluesy walk-up to the tonic.

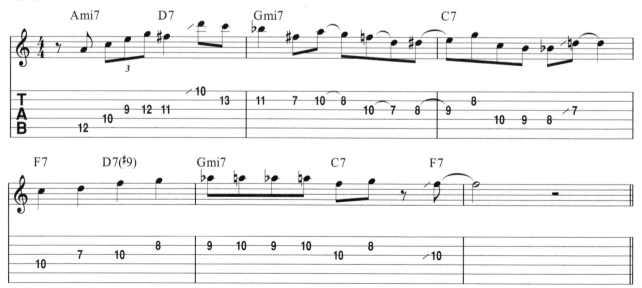

8

Be • low • the • Box Blues

(Cont'd) There are many melodic possibilities in the position below the "box" pattern. As with most rock and blues licks, hammer-ons and pull-offs make this cleaner—and easier to play.

Ben • son • esque

For sheer chops and soul, George Benson has few equals. This homage to the man draws on his R&B roots. It's blues-based, with a flurry of sextuplets that resolve to the downbeat perfectly. Practice this one at a slow tempo to get the timing right.

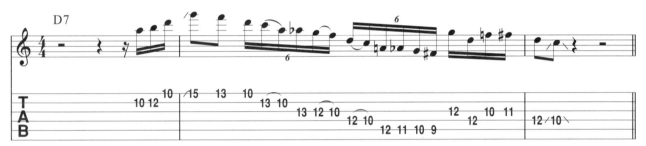

Blue • grass

(Cont'd) Try this on a steel-string acoustic for a real bluegrass sound. It's based around C major pentatonic, but a minor 3rd is added for extra added color. Strive for a clean attack and work this one up to a fast tempo for the right feel.

Blues

Try this phrase out over a V–IV blues change. Use pull-offs for smoothness and speed. This works well in a medium "straight-eighths" feel.

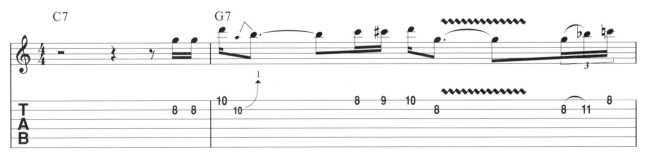

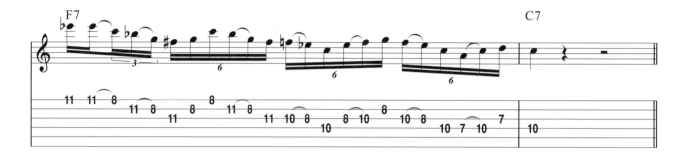

7 Blues Break

(Cont'd) This double-stop lick could be great for stop-time breaks in blues. Try using the fingers on your picking hand instead of a pick.

8 Blues Mix • o • lyd • i • an

Notice how this lick starts off in the typical box position, then adds notes from the Mixolydian mode. It's a good way to get more variation from the five box patterns.

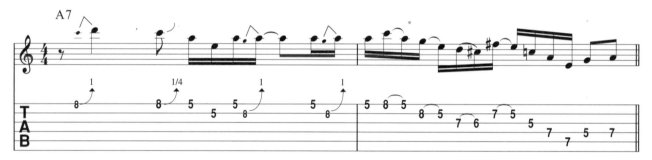

8 Blues • Rock

(Cont'd) This blues-rock lick starts with a bend and combines both major and minor 3rds on a dominant 7th chord. The triplet rhythm makes it well-suited to a shuffle.

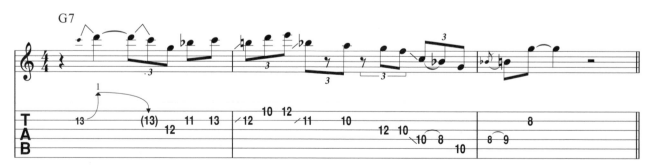

9 Blues Turn • a • round

A classic open-string blues turnaround: Every guitar player should be armed with a vocabulary of these. Use your pick for the bass notes and pluck the descending melody with your second finger.

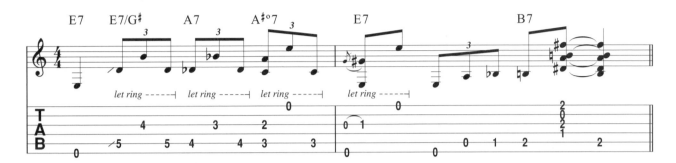

9 Boun • cy Blues
(Cont'd)

This lick has a great rhythmic feel to it. Any triplet-based motif like this works well in a shuffle feel. Using it over a straight-eighth groove creates an interesting duality as well.

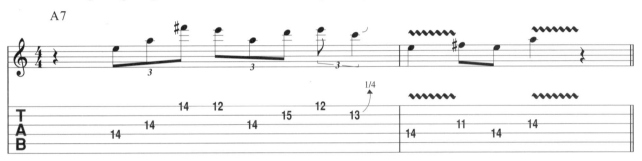

10 Brit • ish Blues

The rhythmic grouping of this lick is interesting. If you accent the G note, the feel of the grouping displaces over the beat. That means the G note keeps popping up in a different place as you loop the phrase.

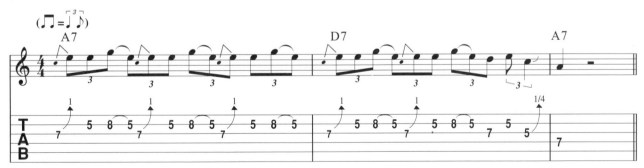

10 Brit • ish Blues
(Cont'd)

This simple-but-elegant lick comes from the Cream era. It could fit over a shuffle or a straight eight.

C

11 Celt • ic

Here's a way to create a 6/8 Irish jig feel. Use a repetitive pull-off to the open G string while maintaining a melody at the same time. Once you get the 6/8 feel, you can start improvising with the notes and developing the motif further. Keep it going! (That's why there are repeats around this one.)

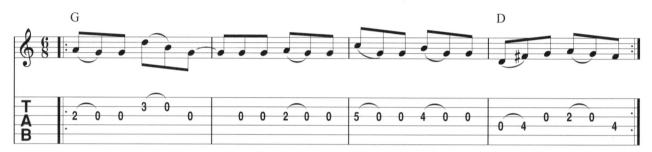

11 (Cont'd) Chi • ca • go Blues

This blues lick has a great rhythmic and melodic feel to it and it extends the box pattern in an interesting way. It's best played over a shuffle. Try moving it to another position for more variation.

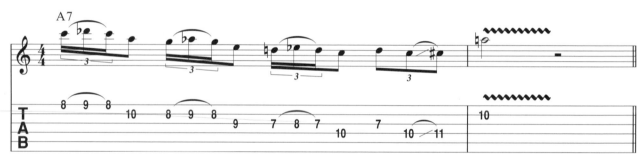

12 Chick • en Pick • in'

This fast country lick is best played with a hybrid right-hand technique using your pick and fingers. The second finger picks the notes on the high E string, while the pick grabs the notes on the second and third strings.

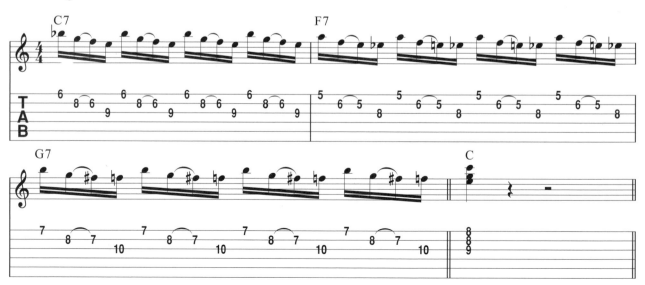

12 Chord Punch • es

(Cont'd) Smooth voice connections make this a nice chord move. The B♭ remains on top as the chords move underneath. Try ending the phrase with a ii–V–I in B♭. (Cmi–F7–B♭ma7). This could be a nice way to end a jazz standard.

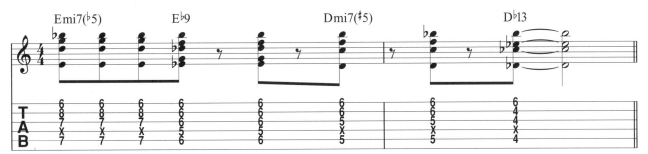

13 Chro • mat • ic Al • tered

Chromatic notes added to the diminished scale can help color a V–I change. Work this one up slowly—the fingering is tricky.

13 Chro • mat • ic Jazz

(Cont'd) This motif slips and slides in and out of the altered dominant 7th chord. Pay attention to the fingering—playing smoothly is vital to the phrasing.

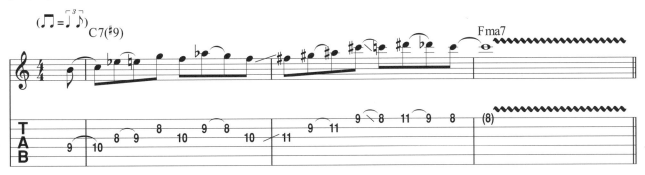

14 Clap • ton • esque

The fast little triplet pull-offs give this lick its classic Clapton sound. This phrase could also work in the box pattern at the twelfth fret.

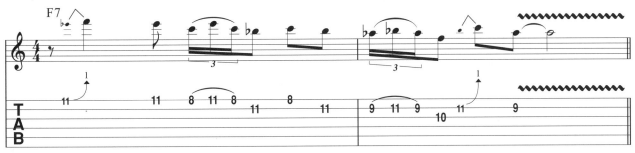

14 Clas • sic Coun • try

(Cont'd) Descending 6th intervals make up this country lick. You can move these down the E and G strings until you end up in first position. Another option is to make a string change on the B♮ (measure 2) to the fourth string and stay in the fifth position. Try both fingerings and figure out which one feels the best.

15 Clas • sic Met • al

Hit the distortion and make full use of your legato technique for this shred-style metal lick. Making use of three notes per string, combined with hammer-ons and pull-offs, it's easy to make this fast and furious.

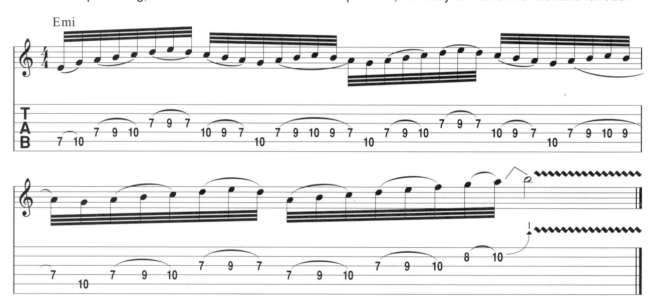

15 Con • trolled Bends

(Cont'd) This lick is just what the name implies. The bends in this case are minor and major thirds. They are harmonic intervals, and care needs to be taken to make sure they are absolutely in tune. The position shifts are tricky as well. As you make the moves down the neck, make sure you control the string noise with left- and right-hand muting.

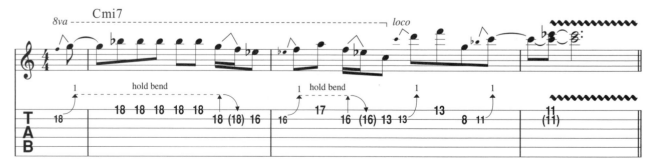

Coun • try

Here's a modern country lick that spreads out the fingers of the left hand in a not-so-conventional way. If you start with your fourth finger on the high D, the fingers end up falling into place rather well.

 ## Coun • try

(Cont'd) This country lick mixes major and minor pentatonic notes. The blend of the major and minor 3rd (E– E♭) is as common in country as it is in rock and blues.

 ## Coun • try

This major pentatonic country lick could be played with pick and fingers for a snappy sound. Make sure the bend is perfectly in tune. The same notes could also work in C# minor.

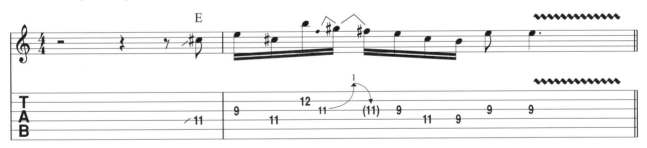

Coun • try End • ing

(Cont'd) This country-flavored lick uses open-string pull-offs. Try using your right-hand fingers for a snappy attack!

18 **Coun • try Rock**

Here's a great-sounding lick loosely based off the sound of two major triads: C and D. The rhythmic phrasing adds musicality. This one works great in blues too!

 18 **Coun • try Rock**
(Cont'd)

Along the same lines as the lick above, these triad ideas give your melodies a wide-open interval feel.

19 **Cropper • ish**

This double-stop riff defines a style associated with much of the classic Stax and Motown R&B records. These partial-chord licks imply the harmony and add melody.

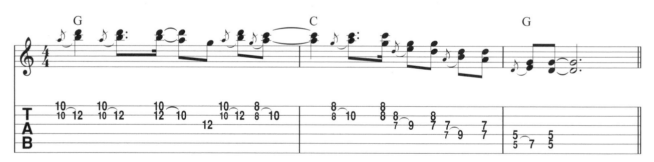

D

 ## Dance
(Cont'd)

Here's a funky little groove that feels good to play. Go for a clean, sharp attack with this rhythm—it's better to make the notes short than long. Knowing all your dominant 7th chord inversions on the top four strings is a must for coming up with on-the-spot grooves. Try this one with a wah-wah.

 ## Di • min • ished Rock

This dominant lick implies altered sounds. After sweeping up the B7 arpeggio, a 4th interval moves in minor 3rds to create an interesting tension.

 ## Di • min • ished Sym • me • try
(Cont'd)

A diminished scale is made up of consecutive half steps and whole steps. The symmetrical feature of this scale provides many interesting patterns for improvising. This lick starts with major 3rds moving up in minor 3rds. In measure 2, it outlines an A7(♭9,♯9) arpeggio and finishes off coming down another pattern.

Dom • i • nant Chord In • ver • sions

These four measures of dominant inversions form a melodic and rhythmic hook. There are many variations that you can make up with them (as on the CD track). Try linking together different combinations to form rhythm guitar grooves.

 Dor • i • an

Here's an interesting Dorian sequence with a passing note. Try it on G7 and Bmi7(♭5). Pull-offs help the phrasing too.

 Dor • i • an

(Cont'd) Notice the use of Diatonic arpeggios that make up this line. The arpeggios are from the key of C, which makes this a Dorian-mode lick.

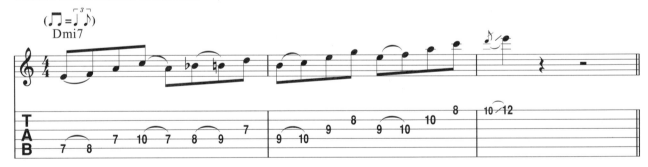

 Dor • i • an In • ter • val

Like the title implies, this lick uses 5ths from the D Dorian mode. It's pretty comfortable in the fifth position as well. To make it smooth, pull off to the indicated notes. Try putting this idea in another position of D Dorian. Could also work over Fma7(♯11).

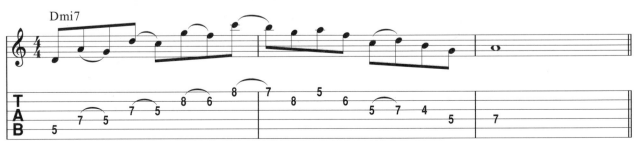

23 Dou • bled Pen • ta • ton • ic
(Cont'd)

This lick is all about the positioning of the slides. Pay attention to the tablature for the fingering.

24 Down • Home Blues

Here's one to play on the front porch with the acoustic. This is one of those licks that always sounds great, because it perfectly outlines the V–IV–I change at the end of the blues.

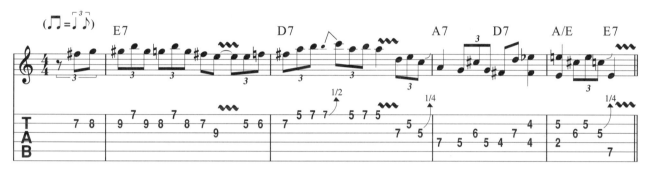

24 Down • Home Blues
(Cont'd)

This is a good example of what's called a "greasy" lick. Check out how the bend from the F♯ up to the A catches the G string underneath with the same finger; this way, you have a reverse bend ready to go. If you do it right, you will release the E back down to the D on the G string. It's a neat effect that gives you that "down-home" sound.

E

 25 Ear • ly Rock 'n' Roll

Right out of the Chuck Berry school: 4th double stops from the pentatonic scale really capture the sound of the early days of Rock 'n' Roll. Try it with all downstrokes.

 25
(Cont'd) **Elec • tric Rock**

Starting with repeat bends, then climbing down the pentatonic scale, this lick is adaptable to many styles. Try it as a blues phrase, or bounce the rhythm and play it as a shuffle.

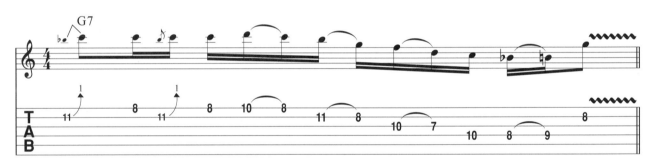

 26 Ex • tend • ed Ar • peg • gio

Here's something I learned from Wes Montgomery. Combining small arpeggios (A♭ major, D diminished, and G major), he creates a beautiful extended type of minor seventh sound. In this case, it's an Fmi13(♭5).

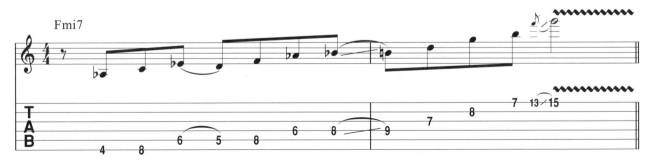

26 Ex • tend • ed Dom • i • nant
(Cont'd)

Here's an arpeggio idea that adds upper extensions to a domininant chord. By spreading out the major and minor 3rd (♯9) across the arpeggio, it conveys the sound of a V7(♯9) more clearly. Try this one with a ♭9 as well.

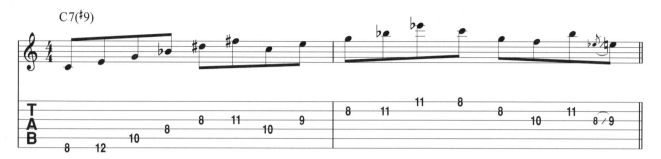

27 End • ing Lick

This is what I mean by "ending lick:" When the band plays the last chord of a tune and it is still ringing, this is a good spot for an improvised line. In this case, the chord should have a dominant 7th sound—although the lick has ♯11 extension in it, a great note for added color. Try this at the end of a blues, with the band holding an A7.

F

27 Fan • cy Blooze
(Cont'd)

This tricky blues lick involves a quick pull-off riff with an extended melody moving up the high E string. Practice this one at a slow tempo. Eventually, you'll be able to turn up the speed when the execution is clean.

28 Fast and Funk • y

This lick, in the style of George Benson, has tricky rhythmic phrasing. Take the time to learn it—a strong rhythm makes a melody even better.

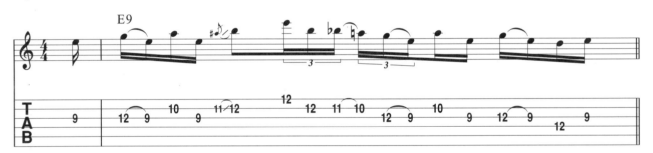

28 Fast Coun • try
(Cont'd)

Here's a double-stop lick that could serve as an ending break on an uptempo country song. It works best when played with a hybrid picking approach. Play with a staccato attack for a crisp sound.

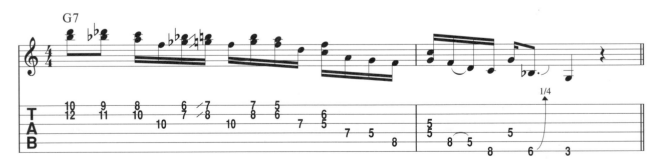

Fast Rock Riff

Here's a lick that needs to burn. It's easy to get it up to speed if you use hammer-ons and pull-offs. Begin slow with just the first measure. Measure 2 is just a variation of the first. Once you get the riff down, it's not as difficult to mix up the pattern with variations.

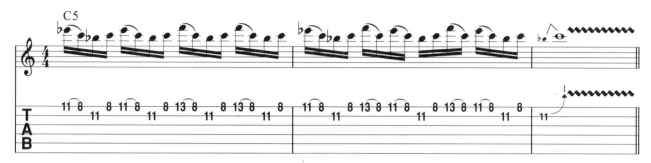

 ## Fin • gers and Pick

This country pickin' lick sounds great when you use the fingers of the right hand with the pick to get a snappy sound—unless, of course, you're left-handed!

 ## Flash • y Blues

This one sounds great when it's played fast and clean. Starting off with a half-step bend, it moves down the scale to end on the minor 3rd. You can give the last note a little bend for extra attitude!

Folk • Rock

There are plenty of acoustic players who don't just strum open G chords. Check out this neat picking idea that adds some nice color. Think of the F♯ and D notes as a C chord shape, up a whole step (without the root). Thanks to James Taylor for great songs and great guitar playing.

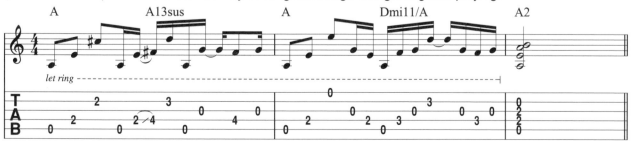

31 Fours in Threes

Making up sequences can be a creative adventure. Here's one that combines a group of four in a pentatonic scale played as triplets, creating an interesting effect. See also Groups of Fives.

31 Funk • y Blues
(Cont'd)

A backwards rake into the first B♭ is essential to making this lick feel funky. The pull-offs smooth it out too. You can use this over E♭7 as well.

32 Fu • sion

This line starts out with two major triads, then finishes with a Mixolydian scale run. Although it moves from twelfth to seventh position, the fingering is actually easiest this way.

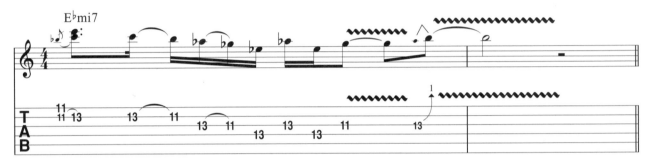

32 Fu • sion Rock
(Cont'd)

Here's a good pentatonic-based lick with major and minor 3rds in it. It sounds best played fast!

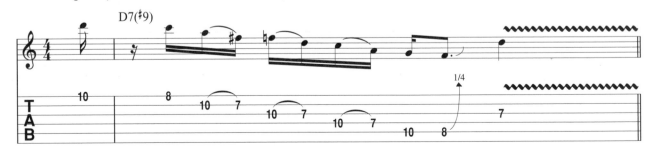

Fu • sion Rock

This lick, in the style of Robben Ford, starts off in a Mixolydian mode, then mutates into straight minor pentatonic.

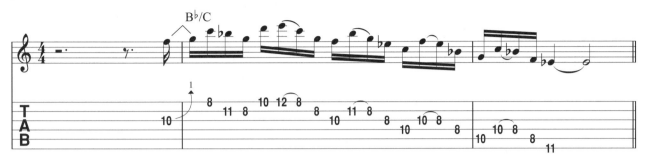

 Fu • sion Rock

(Cont'd) A rock-driven lick is given added dimension with the use of two major triads (B♭ and A) for chromatic tension. These notes add an outside-inside effect.

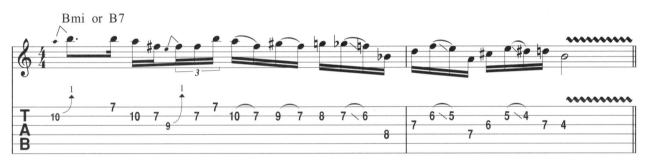

G

Gi • gan • tic Sound

One of the keys to a big sound is low end. That's why this heavy rock lick requires the low E to be dropped down a step to D. By doing this, power chords can be played with one finger! Changing the pitch of a string or two can open the door to new creative possibilities. Warm up the Marshall!

34
(Cont'd) ## Go • in' Off

This rock-blues lick can be played almost entirely with the first and fourth fingers of the fret hand. Using both major and minor 3rds gives it a dominant 7($\sharp$9) feel.

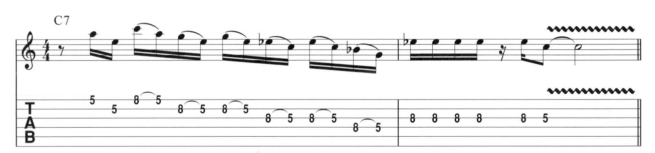

35 ## Groups of Fives

Here's a trick to make your pentatonics sound cool. Play a five-note sequence in a four-note grouping (sixteenth notes). Think of other possibilities. Try a four-note sequence in triplets. (See also "Fours in Threes.")

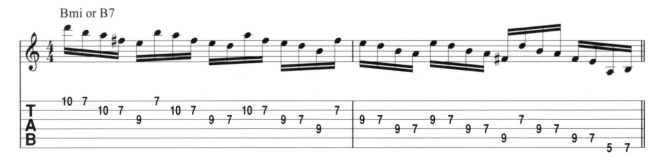

H

35 (Cont'd) **Hard Rock**

Here's a pentatonic-based lick that moves up the neck with slides and triplets. The hammer-ons will help you get it up to speed. Tweak the high A with a slight bend and give the final E some vibrato for extra feel. Rock on!

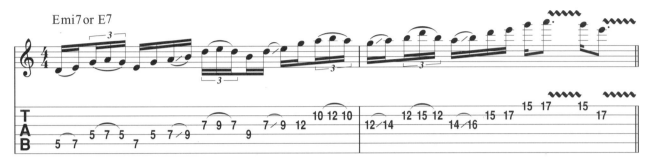

36 **Har • mon • ic Min • or**

Here's a scale that you may be lacking in your vocabulary. The harmonic minor sound comes in handy in a variety of minor-key situations. This lick fits great over a dominant chord that has an implied key center of E minor.

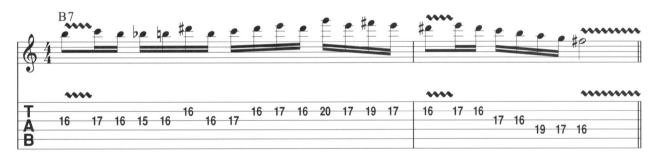

36 (Cont'd) **Heav • y Rock**

This lick starts off with a pull-off in the sixth position and works down to the third position. Sometimes it's better to break licks up into smaller bits when learning them. In this case, work on the phrase up to beat 4, then practice the rest as a second phrase. After doing this, you should find it easier to connect both phrases together.

Heav • y Rock

Crank up the Marshall and rock! This lick, in the style of late-eighties hard rock, fits over a variety of E tonalities: E7, Emi, E7(#9), etc. It can be played over a straight-eighth rock groove or a shuffle feel as well. Try it up an octave too.

Hen • drix • ish

(Cont'd) Dressing up the pentatonic scale with double stops is one of many cool things Jimi did. Reach up with your fourth finger to get the B to ring with the C note. This kind of trick works great for rhythm parts as well. Think of "Little Wing."

High • Tech Rock

This modern-sounding rock lick has some wide interval jumps that make it unique. The shape and sound of these intervals imply the dominant diminished scale. To come up with more of these licks, try studying the way the minor pentatonic scale fits in a diminished scale and add these color notes to your rock licks.

Holds • worth • i • an

(Cont'd) A truly original player, Allan Holdsworth is defined by his brilliant chromaticism and legato technique. Here's one to get you going.

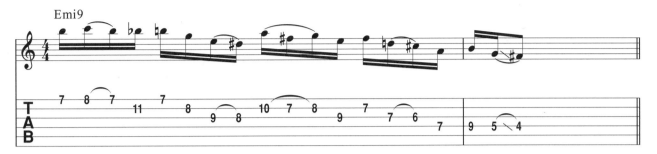

Hy • brid Pick • ing

This is a lick with a lot of potential for other ideas. It utilizes hybrid picking, combining the fingers of the picking hand with the pick. Use your second, third, and fourth fingers to pluck the notes on the G, B, and E strings. This technique takes time to master. Go slowly at first and work up your coordination. Thanks to the amazing Brett Garsed.

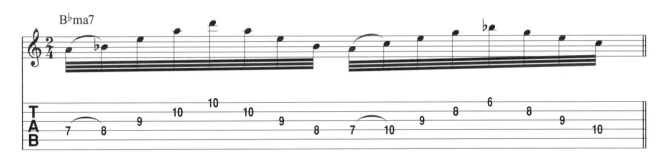

39 In • sane Pent • a • ton • ic
(Cont'd)

This crazy little E minor lick starts off with an unusual pentatonic spread. The notes lay this way to help smooth out the picking for the right hand. Use economy picking when possible. It finishes off with three quick position shifts as it climaxes with a high B pulled off to a G.

40 In • side Out • side

Here's a neat line that goes on a little melody adventure. It starts off with a blues lick, then moves down to B minor and plays a box-position lick. Then, to create an outside sound, the B minor pentatonic slides down to B♭ minor pentatonic. Finally, it slips back down to A minor pentatonic and mixes in some Dorian notes for extra color. Make sure the hammer-ons and pull-offs are in the right spots.

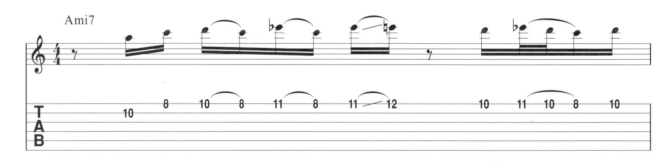

In • ter • val I • de • a

(Cont'd) Here's an idea that really makes you move around the neck. Although it stays completely diatonic, it sounds unique due to the combination of wide intervals and traditional scale steps. Make up some of your own!

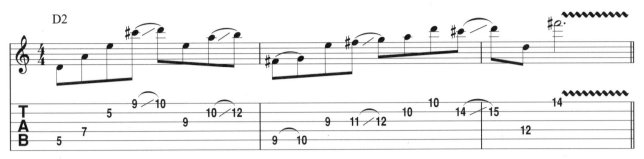

41 I • on • i • an Arp

If you don't know what to play over a major seventh sound, here's a great phrase. It comes right out of a major seventh arpeggio. Using it over Dmi7 will create a beautiful minor 9th sound too.

J

 Jazz Al • tered

(Cont'd) A nice use of intervals and rhythm make this a clever motif.

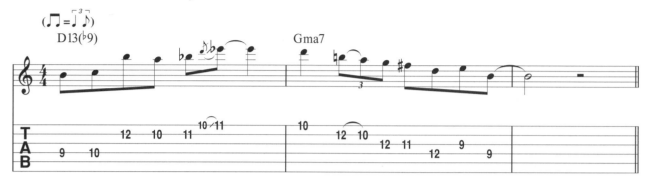

 Jazz • Blues Turn • a • round

This is a double-time phrase that utilizes the melodic minor sound: B♭ melodic minor on the A7 chord and A♭ on the G7 chord. This creates tension notes that tend to pull into the next chord. Thanks to the late great Joe Pass.

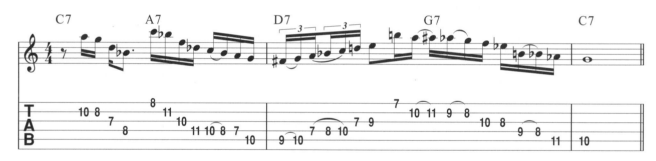

 Jazz • Blues Turn • a • round

(Cont'd) This turnaround melody has a nice shape to it. The descending motif also outlines the chord tones. Experiment with different fingerings too—you have to do this to find out how a melody "lays" the best.

Jazz Sweep

The beginning of this line starts with a downward sweep—make sure the triplet is clean and in time. The rest of the lick is standard alternate picking. This is a nice line for an outside-to-inside resolution on a minor chord.

 Jump Blues

(Cont'd) Here's a neat chordal motif that works well in a lot of blues situations. In the first two measures, let the notes spill into each other for a cascade effect. Then, move up to the tenth position to finish off the rest of the melody. Think of tattoos and Brian Setzer when you play this.

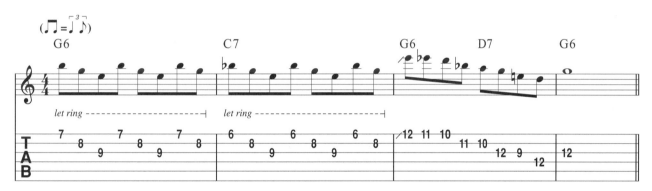

K

 ## Korn • like

Here's a cool one that sounds great with distortion. First, drop the low E to D. It may be easier to read the tab here, as all notes on the E string will be down a step. Check out where the slides are—using them makes the riff groove along better.

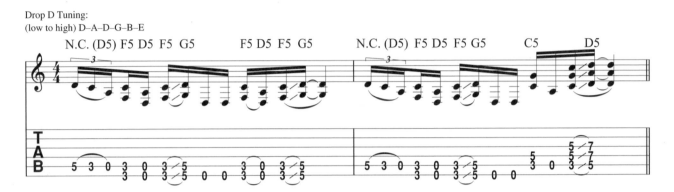

44
(Cont'd)
La • tin Rock

Start with a downward sweep to play the D minor triad, then bend the first note of each half-note triplet. This one has a lot of Santana in it.

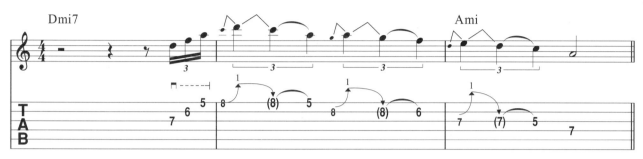

45
Le • ga • to

Check out the heavy use of chromatic notes in this lick. The neat thing is how you can still hear the sound of the A Dorian mode in the line. Pay careful attention to the slurs!

45
(Cont'd)
Lou • is • i • an • a Blues

The key of E is made for the guitar, and this lick exemplifies that. Droning the high E string while playing a melody on the B string gives this lick an authentic old blues flavor. There are many variations in the open E position.

46
Ly • di • an Ar • peg • gi • o

This is a fun little shape that climbs up the neck with a Lydian sound. It includes the use of the major 7th arpeggio with the added ♯11 spread out over two octaves.

M

46
(Cont'd) ## Ma • jor ii • V • I

This line starts out with an Fma7 arpeggio over the Dmi7. On the V chord, you have a nice descending line that captures the color of a ♭9, ♯9, and ♯5.

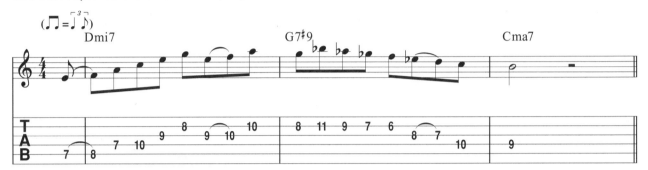

47 ## Mar • ti • no • Like

This is a double-time ii-V-I lick. It starts with a smooth minor 7th lick, then walks down the D and G strings. Once your left hand is in fifth position, the rest of the line falls into place.

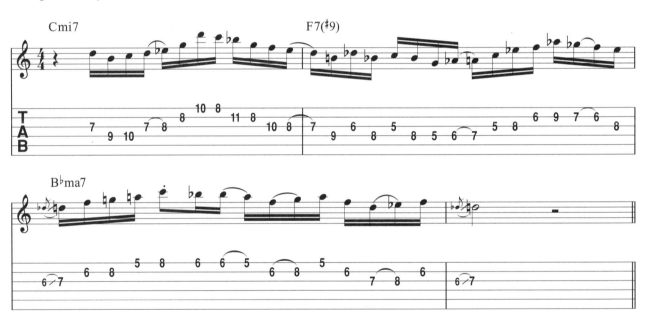

47
(Cont'd) ## Me • lod • ic Mi • nor

This jazzy altered dominant line extends the natural tension in a V7 dominant by using the melodic minor up a half step from the chord. It also does so in a melodic way—with interesting intervals.

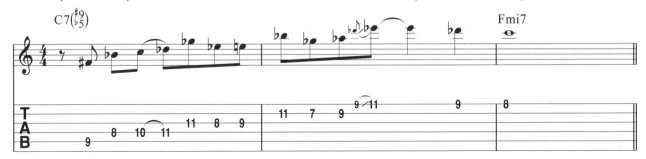

36

48 Me • lod • ic Mi • nor

This very useful melody comes straight out of the E♭ melodic minor scale. A melodic minor scale played up a half step from the dominant chord creates the sound we also call the altered scale.

48 Met • al
(Cont'd)

This ripping lick takes advantage of the "box-position extension"—when you extend the four-fret span to a six-fret span on the top string. Finding new ways to lay your hands over the same old patterns is a good way to come up with new stuff. Play this one with a lot of pull-offs.

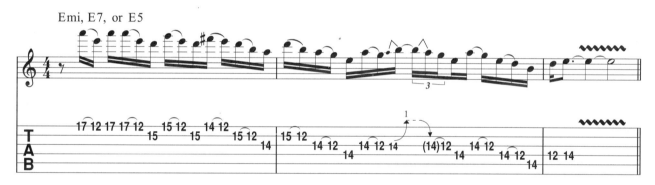

49 Metheny • Like

Here's a chromatic jazz lick that uses hammer-ons and slides. This kind of picking, very much a part of the Metheny style, can increase your speed and legato feel.

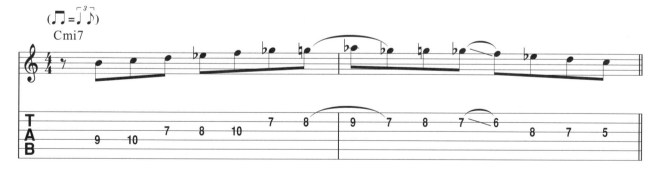

Minor ii • V • I
(Cont'd)

Here's an elegant double-time lick, in the style of Mike Stern, that fits a minor cadence. It starts with one-octave arpeggios of A♭ma7 and Dmi7(♭5). It then moves down the E string with a smooth chromatic line that colors the dominant chord—check out the fingering on this part. Finally, it finishes up with a diminished scale and resolves to the 9th of the i chord.

 Mi • nor Sev • enth

This jazzy minor idea has added interest due to the chromatics. A short lick like this is possible in many different positions. This is a good starting point for a Metheny-type sound.

 Mix • o • lyd • i • an Mix
(Cont'd)

Notice how this line smoothly connects the sound of D Mixolydian to an E7 sound. A strong downbeat chord-tone resolution on the E helps the connection.

51 Mod • ern Blues

This eighth-position lick starts with a fourth-finger bend. The second note is the same pitch. Make sure your bend is a perfect whole step. Pull-offs help smooth the phrasing on the way back down.

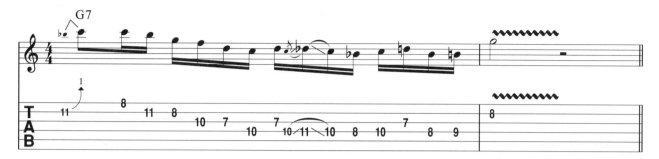

51 Mod • ern Rock

(Cont'd) This rock lick starts below the box position and moves down one more. Try working out a few different fingerings. Moving through positions can be tricky, so start slowly before trying it up to speed.

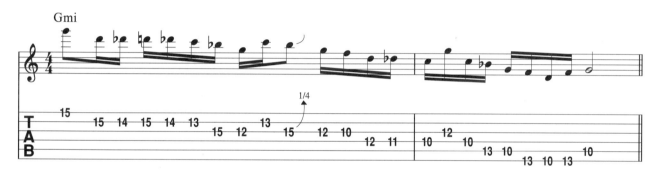

52 Mo • town Rhyth • m

Thanks to Steve Cropper for this great funky E7 groove. This kind of part works best when the bass groove has open holes in it. That way, the low end-heavy rhythm fills in the spaces without getting in the way. Check out the original, "Knock on Wood."

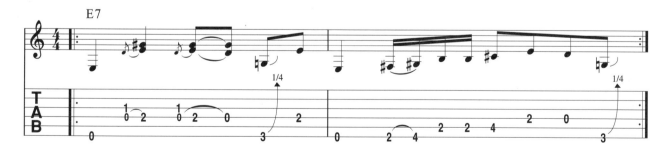

N

52 Near • ly Blues

(Cont'd) Okay, this lick doesn't sound like something B.B. would play, but you can still use it over a blues. The wide-open intervals give this phrase a modern sound. Could also fit over Emi7(♭5).

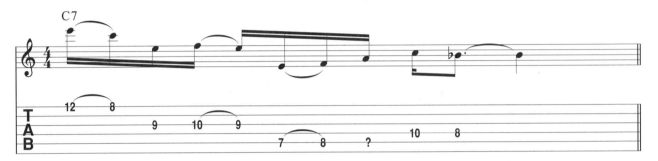

53 Near • ly Dor • i • an

A modal lick doesn't have to stay completely diatonic to fit in that mode. Examine this line to see how the use of chromatic passing tones added to arpeggios can enhance the Dorian sound. The secret is the placement of the chromatic notes; avoid playing them on downbeats. This lick is reminiscent of a Robben Ford idea.

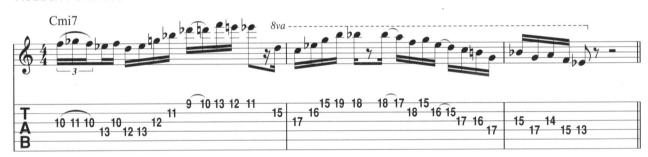

53 New Age

(Cont'd) Here's one borrowed from the classic composers. The concept starts with a pedal (in this case C). Then the melody works down the scale while pedaling the high C. It finishes with a simple resolution to the I.

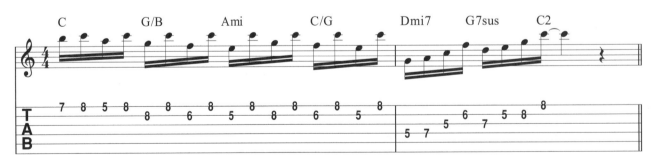

40

54 New Age

This could sound really nice with some delay and chorus. Make sure you stay out of the way of the low E as it's ringing. It supports the key center as you play the melody on the top three strings.

54 New Age A • cous • tic
(Cont'd)

This jangly-sounding chord riff makes a nice ending for an acoustic piece in E. Allow the notes to ring together as much as possible, and pay attention to the open strings—the low E should ring through the first measure. This lick is best played with a fingerpicking approach.

55 Ninth Chord Run

This lick can be used on any non-functioning dominant chord. Although it uses chromatic notes for added color and melody, notice how the chord tones land on the downbeats, making the line retain the sound of the harmony clearly.

O • pen Sounds

(Cont'd) The term "open" in music can refer to many things—in this case, the spacing of intervals. There are many wide intervals utilized in this phrase. Notice the use of 5ths in the beginning and octave jumps at the end.

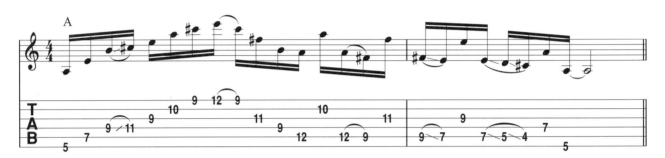

 O • pen String End • ing

Watch the tab on this one. The idea here is to use open strings in a descending melody to create a cascading harp-like effect. This one could sound good as an ending to an acoustic piece.

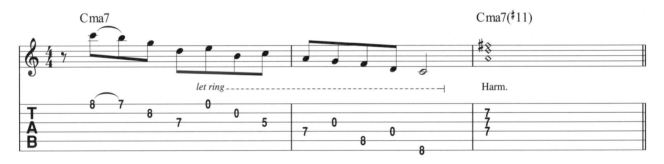

 Out • side Loop

(Cont'd) Try looping this lick over and over, and note how the phrasing turns around. You can move it in minor 3rds as well, because all the notes fit in the diminished scale. (Shapes in this scale can move in minor 3rds and remain diatonic.)

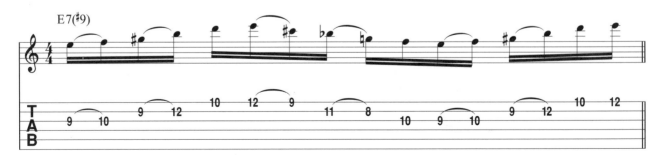

P

57   Pat • tern for Dor • i • an

Playing this line smoothly takes a little practice. It helps to incorporate legato fingering. To completely master this, try starting the pattern from any note in the C Dorian scale. Use your ear to negotiate the chromatic notes.

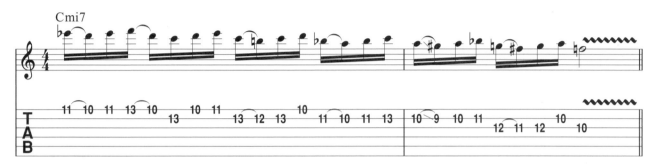

57   Ped • al Steel
(Cont'd)

Watch your intonation on these bends. Hold the G with the high C♯ and add a little vibrato for a pedal-steel effect.

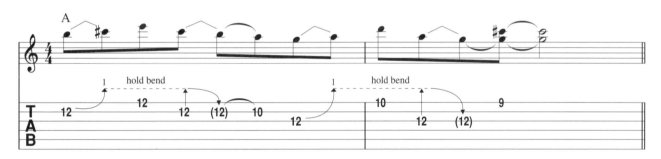

58   Pen • ta • ton • ic Shift • ing

Here's a speedy rock lick that moves through the A minor pentatonic patterns with a rhythmic figure. Pay attention to the legato fingerings and the placement of the slides.

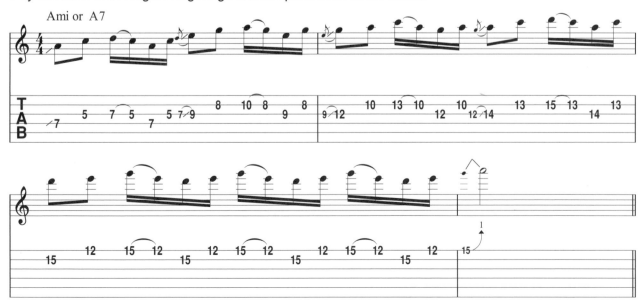

Phry • gian
(Cont'd)

The Phrygian mode always gives an exotic flavor to a minor chord. Place this in the seventh position and utilize hammer-ons and pull-offs for a legato sound. The emphasis is on the ♭2 of the scale (in this case, B♭).

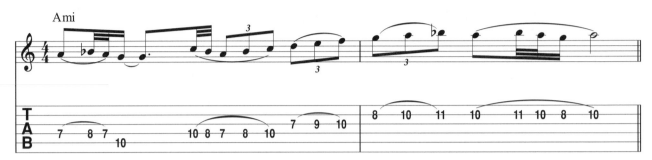

 ## Po • si • tion Shift • er

Notice how this pentatonic-based lick connects the neck with slides. Using this technique gives you more possibilities than staying in the box pattern. Sliding also gives your phrasing a different feel.

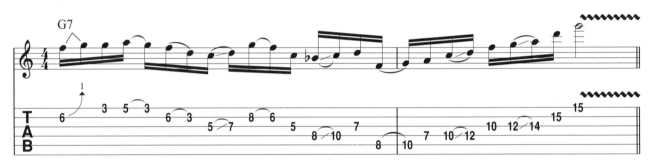

 ## Pow • er Pop
(Cont'd)

Catchy guitar hooks are the basis of many a pop hit. One of the tricks to composing a part is incorporating a melody in a chordal riff. This lick has a cool rhythmic feel to it and creates a melodic hook with the notes on top of the chords. Make up some of your own.

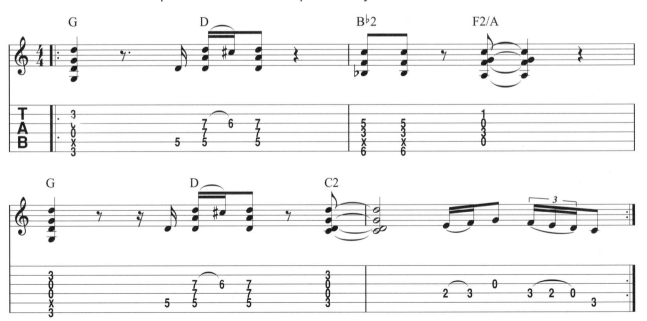

Pro • gres • sive Rock

This lick starts with a four-note phrase, moves up one octave and then one more with a variation. On the second high D, pre-bend it from a C♯, so you can release it to the C♯. This is a cool way to imply a sus4 dominant sound.

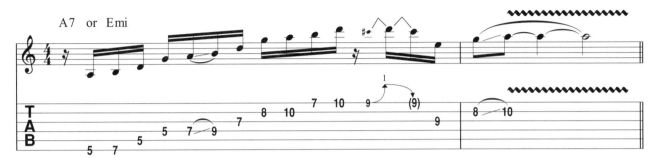

Psy • che • del • ic

(Cont'd)

This is a great stylistic lick if you're trying to capture the feel of a sitar. By using open strings in the first position, you can create a cascading effect. Make sure the notes run together as a chord. This could also work over a C♯mi7 chord (as a ii chord). Far out!

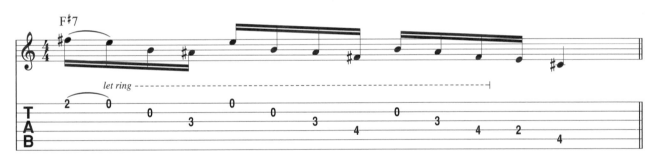

Q

61 Quar • tal Chord Lick

The idea behind this chord movement is quite interesting. The melody on top is moving down an E minor pentatonic scale. The notes underneath that fall on the downbeats of 1, 2, 3, and 4 form G, F, E♭, and C triads. However, the notes on the upbeats are a half step below each triad, forming a perfect 4th stack. Although it may seem a little atonal at first, it sounds great over Emi7 or E7(♯9). This is a classic Miles Davis trick.

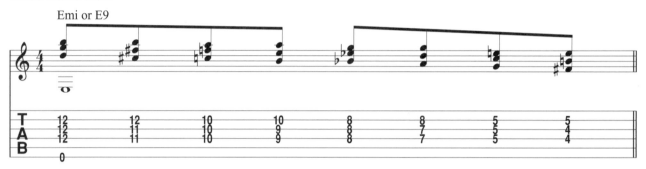

61 Ques • tion and An • swer Lick
(Cont'd)

This one is right out of the call-and-response style of great blues playing. Try playing it on the first four measures of a blues. Think "slowhand."

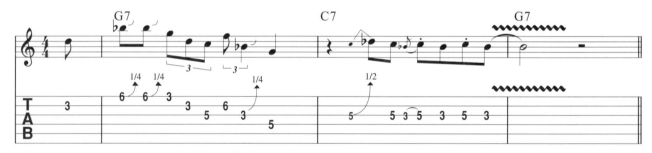

62 Quick Lick

This lick is simple, but it sure feels good to play. The rhythmic motif fits perfectly in a shuffle. This one will work great on the last two measures of an A blues.

62 (Cont'd) Quirk • y Blues

The hammer-ons and slides in this phrase help smooth out the melodic jumps. This could work in rock, blues, or fusion. If it's too long to work with, try just using the first seven notes.

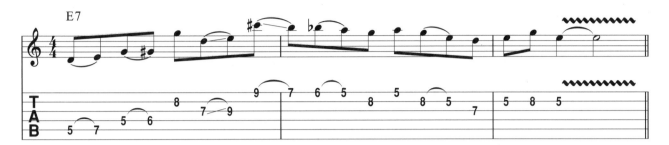

63 Quirk • y Rock

Here's a cool rock/blues lick that starts with an open kind of angular shape and moves it up a whole step. Although it's based on minor and major pentatonics, it has a unique sound.

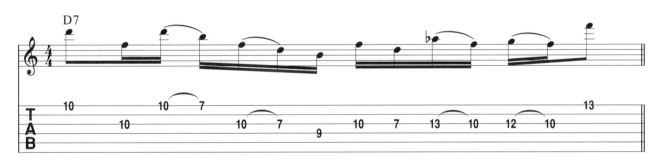

R

63 (Cont'd) ## Rag • time

The 6th and 3rd intervals combined give this phrase a Scott Joplin-esque Ragtime feel. Try it with hybrid picking or just plain fingers. It sounds great on an acoustic!

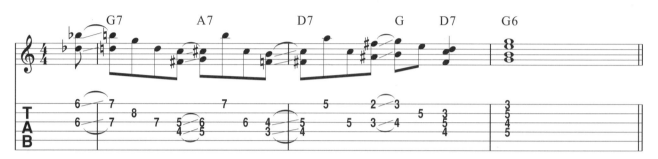

64 ## Rap • id Bends

One of the great things about the guitar is the many different ways you can play a note. This lick demonstrates two approaches. By rapidly alternating between a fretted and bent D, released to a C#, you create an interesting effect. And because it's a three-note pattern, it creates an odd-against-even (sixteen notes to a beat) effect.

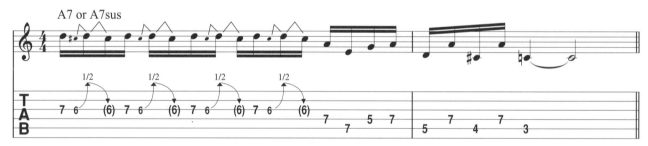

64 (Cont'd) ## Reg • gae

Dial in a bright, clean tone for this rhythm groove. Notice how a simple melody is implied. Creating melodies in rhythm parts is important in all styles, especially reggae. Make sure you swing the rhythm. Ya man!!

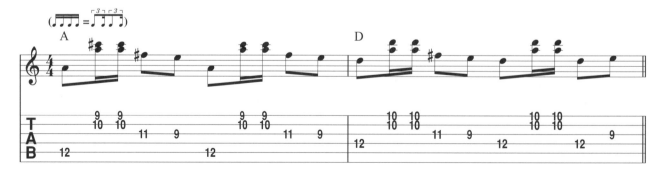

R

 ## Ret • ro

Here's a neat double-stop blues riff. This could work as an ending break in a blues. The notes in parentheses are ghost noes, to be played very lightly.

 ## Rhyth • mic Rock
(Cont'd)

This simple bending blues lick has a great rhythmic feel to it. Try transposing it to other patterns too.

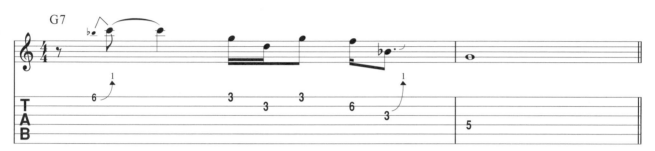

 ## Rhyth • mic Rock

The timing on this is tricky. Sometimes the difference between a typical lick and an exceptionally cool one is the rhythm. The delayed feel of the bends, mixed with the sixteenth notes and the triplets, make this lick less predictable and more interesting.

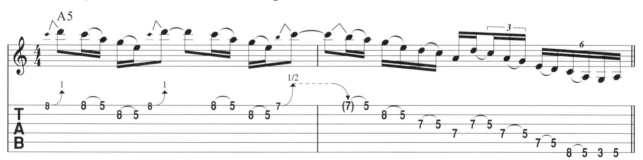

Riffs

Every rock/blues player needs to have a basic vocabulary of riffs at his/her command. A *riff* is a motif, usually three to seven notes long, played in a series of repetitions. The following three riffs are great for adding intensity to any solo—especially when played uptempo.

Riff #1

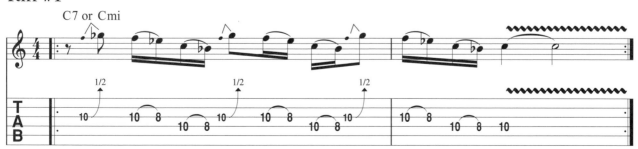

Riff #2

This riff creates a cool accent when looped. Use pull-offs for faster execution.

Riff #3

This one has a flashy rhythm feel. It's good for a solo climax builder.

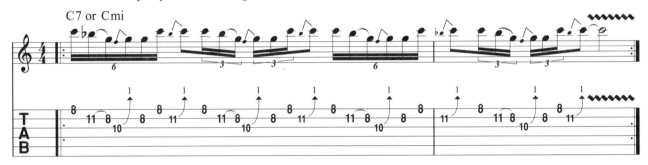

 ## Rock • a • bill • y

Go for a twangy sound and crank up the reverb on this lick. It's a good example of Carl Perkins-style country swing—the backbone of rockabilly.

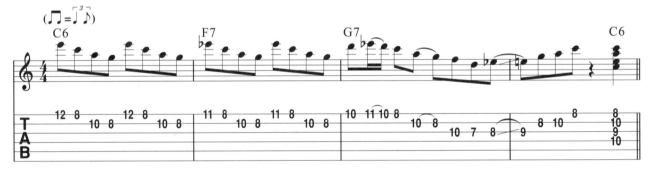

68 (Cont'd) ## Rock and Roll Rhyth • m

Working from a fifth-position C major pentatonic shape allows for a variety of classic rock 'n' roll rhythms. Underneath the four-fret span are the major and minor 3rds, plus the 6th and ♭7th degrees. Beginning with the root and mixing up the notes in a melodic way captures the essence of early rock 'n' roll. I call this position the "Stones Box."

Rock Blues

This is a good lick for a shuffle or straight-eighth feel. It fits that position right above the familiar box pattern.

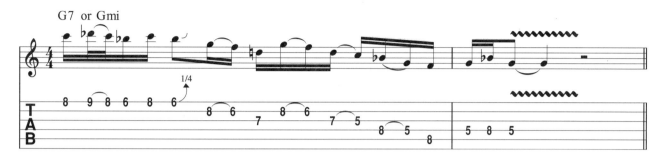

 Roots • y Rock

(Cont'd)

Double stops give this phrase a country flavor. Notice how the thirds stay diatonic to the dominant seventh chords. It may feel the best played on the top two strings as long as possible.

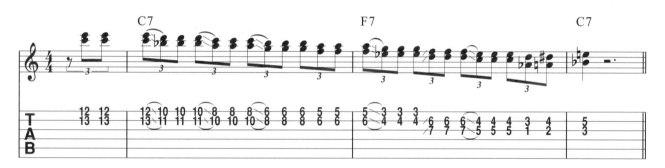

S

70 Sax Sounds

This line comes right from the vocabulary of classic saxophone motifs. The concept at work here is the target approach to the chord tones (preceding chord tones by notes above or below). It can work over a dominant chord (G7) as well.

70 Sco Sounds
(Cont'd)

This contemporary jazz-fusion line has a lot going on. It starts off implying a B♭ dominant diminished scale up to the F. Then, to add tension, the line seems to imply an F7 altered chord (the V of B♭), resolving back to B♭ on the final F. This is a common device in the jazz vocabulary. Thanks to John Scofield for this one.

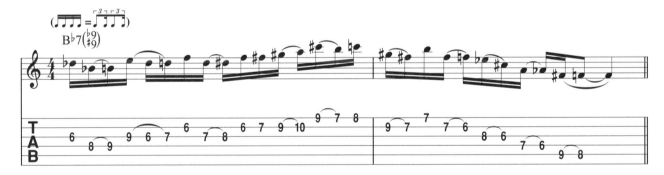

71 Ska

Like its reggae cousin, ska music originated in Jamaica. Where a reggae groove is more laid back, ska is usually more upbeat. Play the eighth upbeats as sharp, clean upstrokes and go for a crisp, clear sound. Remember the English Beat?

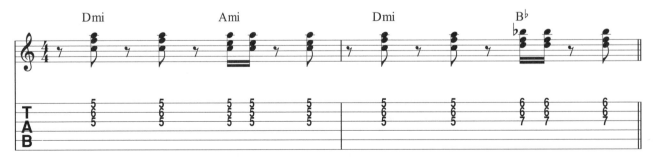

Slick Blues
(Cont'd)

This one has a lot of grease behind it. To get the right slick feel, try a backwards "rake" down to the first low A note—right out of Robben Ford's bag of blues.

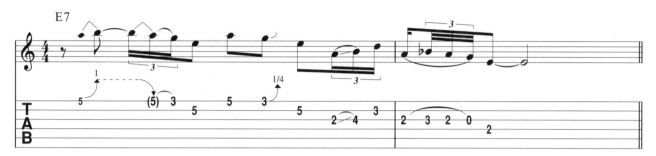

Slide Mel • o • dy

This is a simple melody, but getting the intonation right is always tricky.

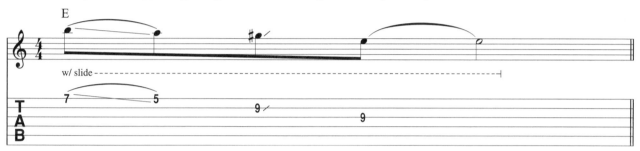

Slide Mel • o • dy
(Cont'd)

This one has that "down-home" feel to it. Good intonation is always a must with slide phrases. Play the fretted notes a few times to get the melody in your ear, then incorporate the slide. Disconnect some of the notes for a more distinctive rhythm.

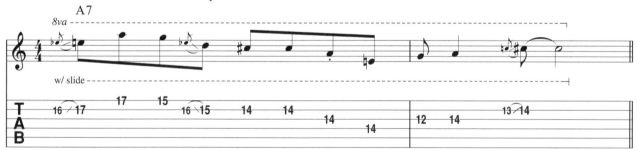

Slide Mel • o • dy

This one takes practice to get smooth and clean. Notice the use of the open G string throughout the phrase. You must develop a delicate touch when bringing the slide on and off the strings; you don't want to create any extra fret/string noise. It's best to use the fingers on the right hand for precise muting technique.

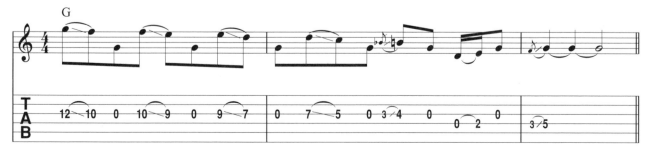

Slid • ing and Bend • ing
(Cont'd)

This line combines slides and bends to connect positions. The major 6th in the melody indicates that it's a Dorian-mode lick. Efficient use of your fingers is important in this lick. Start the A with your third finger. When you move up to the high D, use your first finger. Finally, bend the E up to the D with your third finger.

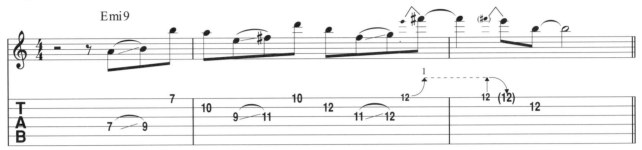

 ## Smooth and Fast

This one is spread out across two strings to maximize speed and smoothness. The fist four notes are picked once, then the B on the B string is plucked with the middle finger. Look for other ways to incorporate the fingers of your picking hand for extra speed in your lines.

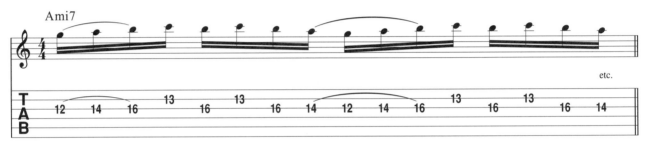

 ## Smooth Jazz
(Cont'd)

What do you call jazz with all the rough edges polished off? Smooth! It's a style typified by nice easy melodies over mellow inside harmonies. This lick could work perfectly when you have a IV chord moving down to a iii. Practice making the legato line connect seamlessly. Try it with a clean tone.

 ## Smooth Slides

This lick is made up of diatonic 3rds sliding through three positions on adjacent strings. You can let the last 3rds ring together with the high D to form a chord.

Soul • ful Bend • ing
(Cont'd)

Here's a neat bending lick that gives you a new slant on a blues-rock sound. The positioning of the left hand is important. Bending the final A up to B is difficult on the D string—make sure you're up to pitch!

Soul • ful R • & • B

This lick repeats in two octaves, then finishes off with a blues kind of phrase. Think of this in the jazz/R&B style of the great George Benson.

South • ern Rock
(Cont'd)

This one comes right out of the Dickey Betts school. It starts with a whole-step bend and stays in C major pentatonic. Slides are thrown in to help keep it interesting.

String Slid • er

This lick starts off in a typical position, then uses slides to bridge to the next position. The chromatic notes add tension.

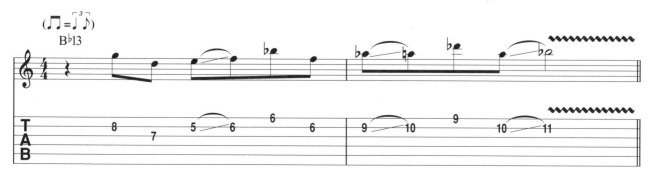

77 **Sus • pend • ed Dom • i • nant Ar • peg • gi • o**
(Cont'd) Taking an arpeggio and modifying one note can make a remarkable difference in the sound. Here, we start off with an A7 arpeggio in seventh position and suspend the major 3rds of the arpeggio. This creates a much more "open" feel.

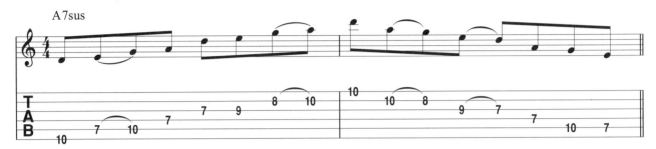

 78 **Surf**

Dial in a bright tone with a lot of reverb for this surf-inspired lick. Pick the notes hard and close to the bridge for a true Dick Dale feel.

 78 **Swing**
(Cont'd) Here's a bebop jazz lick that just feels great over a ii–V–I progression. This is what you might call a classic jazz motif à la Sonny Rollins.

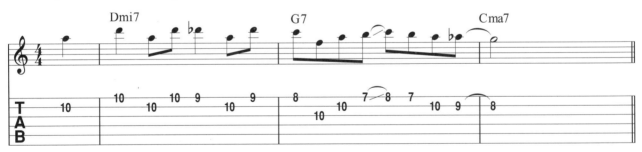

 79 **Sym • met • ry**

Here's another one from the diminished scale, taking full advantage of the symmetry. In this case, we have minor 3rds ascending in major 3rds. It's interesting to note how this line seems to fit over three minor chords. Although using the diminished scale over these minor chords creates chromatic notes, they are acceptable "colors" that sound good.

79 (Cont'd) Tech • nic • al Rock

This hot rock lick fits in the blues box and makes use of repeated bends to the root. As you work your way down the pattern, you pick up extra notes for color—in this case, the major 6th and the ♭5th. Watch the timing on the sextuplets. The last G should be landing just before the downbeat of 4.

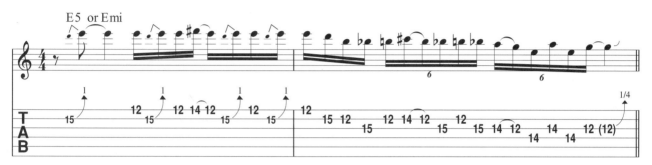

80 Texas Blues

Play this one with lots of Texas attitude. Try raking into the first note.

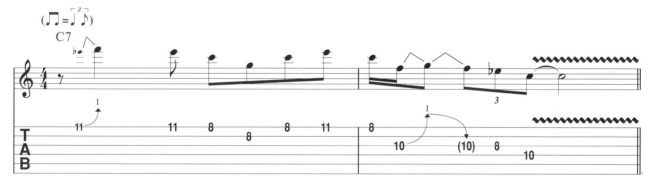

80 (Cont'd) Trav • is Pick • ing

Pick up the acoustic for this one. There are many variations of this fingerpicking style. Note the way the bass alternates between the root and the 5th. Once you master these patterns in a variety of chord forms, it becomes easy to chain them together into a song.

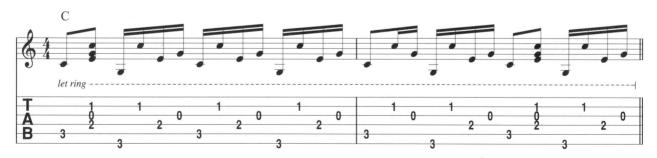

81 Trip • let Blues

Dig the way this one moves from the IV chord to the I chord of a blues progression. Three consecutive triplets make it perfect for a shuffle. Try using the fingers of your picking hand for a bright, snappy sound.

81 Trip • let Rock
(Cont'd)

Here's a great lick that makes use of triplets. Starting off with an in-your-face double stop, it moves into a series of triplets (sextuplets) in the familiar box pattern. After climbing up the pattern, it extends up to the sus4 (G) before resolving to the ♭7. Another lick in the style of the great Robben Ford.

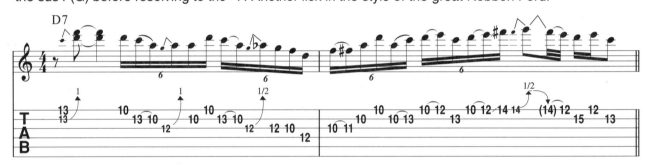

82 Tri • ton • al

Looking for a lick that sounds a little different? Check out this diminished idea. The four major triads in this scale (E, G, B♭, and D♭) are hooked together to form an intervallic altered dominant lick. Try them in different combinations. This can be moved in minor 3rds and still fit the chord.

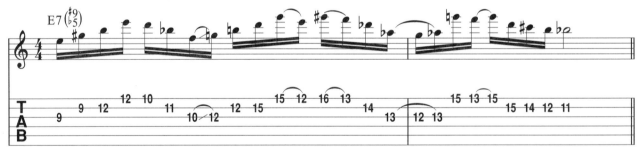

82 Tri • tone Twang
(Cont'd)

This country-flavored lick is loosely based on the idea of combining triads a ♭5th apart. The triads are not literally played, they are implied. In this case, G and D♭ are used. This could work well in an uptempo blues-based country tune.

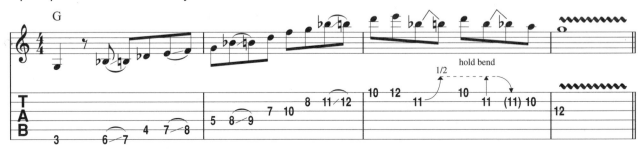

58

Twang • y Thirds

This double-stop lick could work well in country or blues. Make sure you watch the bends, and pay careful attention to the intonation.

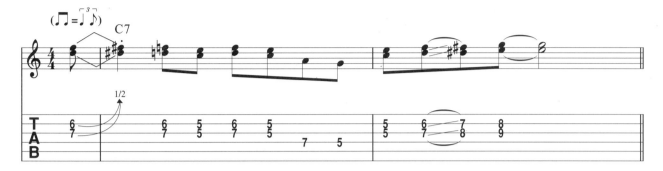

 ## Two • Hand Tapping

(Cont'd)

This tapping lick may take a while to work out, so start slowly. It begins with a bend from the D up to the E. Then you tap the fourteenth fret with your right hand. After you release the tap, release the bend back to D and while it's still ringing, bend right back up to E. This pattern continues as you tap down the G string. It ends with a series of tapped 16th-note triplets.

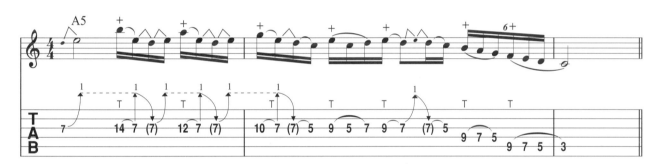

Two Tri • ads

The idea in this line is the use of a G augmented triad and an A major triad. This two-triad approach creates an upper-structure sound to an A7 chord—A9(#5).

U

84 (Cont'd) ## Un • i • dent • i • fied Fly • ing Fin • gers

Breaking up the box position with some leaping finger jumps is the main purpose of this lick. Use consecutive downstrokes until you come back to the A on the B string. Whenever you fall prey to that "same old lick" syndrome, try incorporating wider intervals in your licks for some fresh ideas. You'll be amazed at what you can invent.

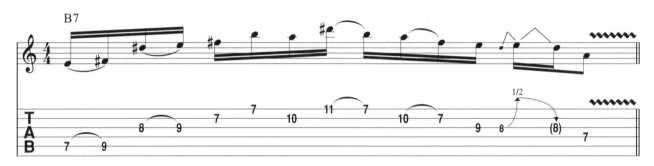

Un • us • u • al Bend • ing

Although this lick may look simple at first, pay careful attention to the fingers you use to bend. When releasing to the B♭ from B with your fourth finger, catch the A with your third finger. Then you're ready to bend the G with your first finger. Thanks to Sonny Landreth.

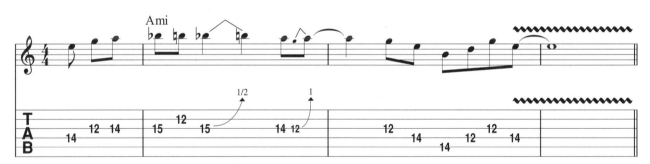

85 (Cont'd) ## U • til • i • ty Jazz

Notice the use of arpeggios mixed in with the Dorian-mode notes. Make sure you get the hammer-ons and slides in the right places.

◆86 U • til • i • ty R&B

Here's a classic staple of R&B, soul, and funk. Double stops in diatonic 4ths can be an interesting way to add melody to a rhythm part. The intervals tend to sound ambiguous and therefore can fit over many chords in the diatonic scale. Experiment with this lick over other chords in the key of E major.

Van Hal • en • esque

(Cont'd) Here's a classic from tapping master Eddie Van Halen. After working your way down the B string, you have to jump down to the G string to continue. Then you keep hopping down until you get to the low E. It takes practice to make this smooth. Try breaking this lick up into two sections, then combining them.

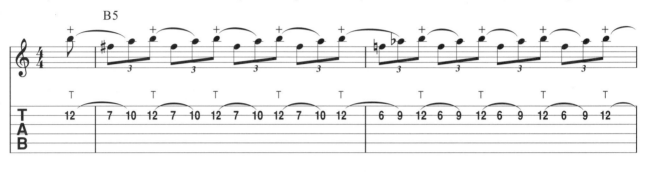

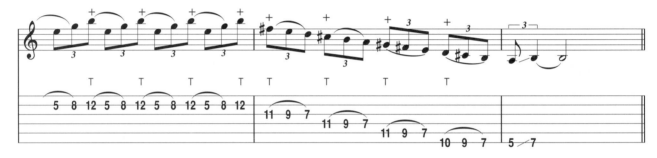

 Vaughan • like

This blues lick drips with heartache. Start off with a whole-step bend from the E to the F♯. Then, with your first finger, bend the D up to the E for more anguish. (This is a tough bend, especially with heavy strings.) After the bends, move down to seventh position and finish it off with a box-pattern phrase. This man had a feel!

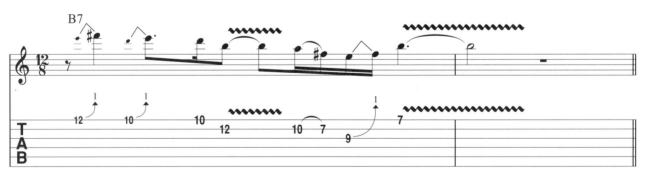

62

Vaughan, Stev • ie Ray
(Cont'd)
This is one soulful blues lick. The timing may look weird—once you learn the fingering, copy the rhythm with your ear. It works great in a slow 12/8 blues, à la "Texas Flood."

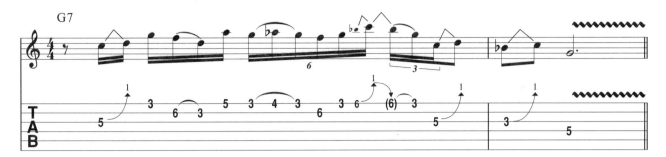

 Ver • y Smooth
Check out the fingering on this dominant-7th lick. It's important to start on the B♭ with your third finger. On the double F, use your thirrd finger as well to make it smooth.

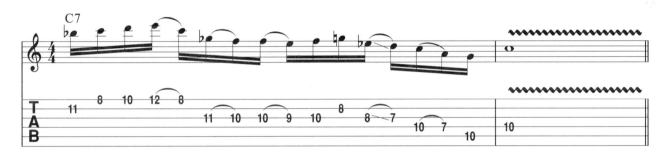

 Vin • tage Rock
(Cont'd)
A variation of the "flashy blues" lick on track 30. To give this lick extra attitude, hit the low C hard and slide into it.

89 Wes • Like

This graceful ii–V–I lick is in the style of the great Wes Montgomery. Notice the smooth way it resolves to the 6th of the E♭ chord. Mastering note resolution is one of the secrets of jazz.

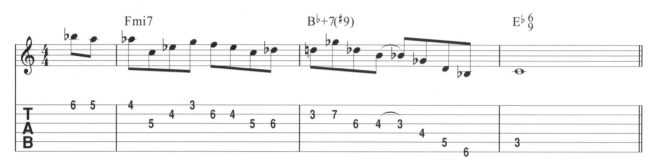

89 (Cont'd) Wes • Like ii • V • I

Here's another neat lick inspired by Wes Montgomery. The idea is to use a ♭5 sub over the B♭7 chord—in other words, playing an E♭7 sound as a substitute for the B♭7.

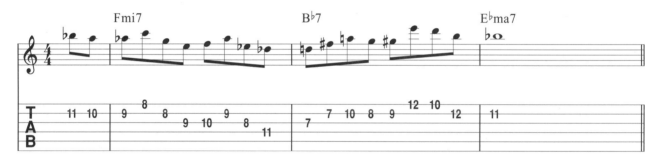

90 West • Coast Blues

Notice how the second measure of this blues-based lick is nearly identical to the first; this is a technique you can use to make up your own licks.

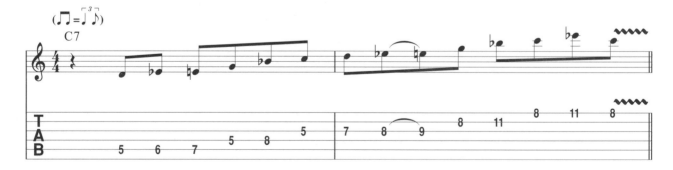

West Coast Cool

(Cont'd) This jazz phrase starts with a graceful sweep, then moves down the D string chromatically. When you hit the A note, you'll mix in chromatics from the A string as well. Finally, you reach fourth position and imply an E9 for a resolution. This one is very Benson-esque.

 ## Wide O • pen Spac • es

The "open" sound of this lick is due to the large intervals at work. It also incorporates F and G triads to create a G9sus sound. It could also fit an Fmaj7.

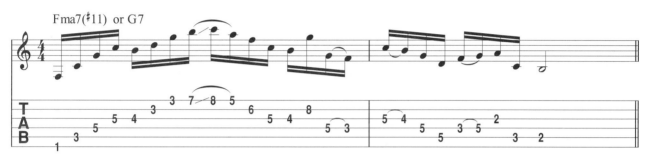

 ## Whole Tone

(Cont'd) What do you get when you play six consecutive whole steps? The aptly-named *whole tone* scale. Its special sound is best used over dominant chords that have a flatted or sharp 5th and a natural 9th. In this whole-tone lick, the four-note groupings of eighth notes make the three-note phrase of the lick displace in an interesting way.

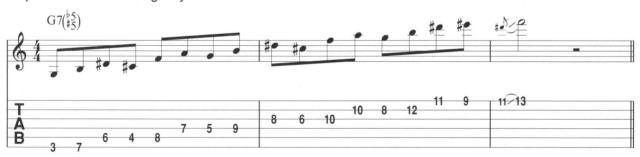

 ## Whole Tone

Here's a three-note sequence whole-tone lick that ascends in major 3rds.

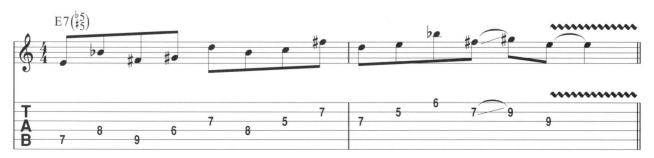

92 (Cont'd) Whole Tone Riff

The whole tone scale can provide some interesting sounds. Here's one that starts off with a double-stop lick, then moves it up a step and down a step, respectively. This lick could fit over any dominant chord built off any note of the scale (A7, B7, C♯7, D♯7, F7, or G7).

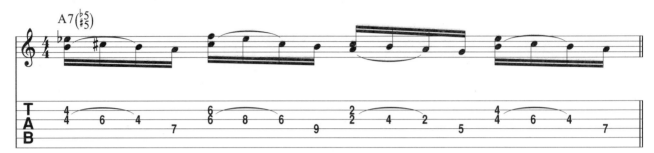

93 World Beat

This bright, happy rhythm typifies the feel of a lot of world-beat guitar parts, usually based around major pentatonic melodies and played with a clean tone. Often, a muting technique is employed. The harmonies are typically simple, as in this example, moving from a I chord to a V chord.

94   X • tend • ed Dom • i • nant

This lick seems to be playable almost exclusively with the first and third fingers. Make sure you slide where indicated. Thanks to Larry Carlton for this one.

94   X • tend • ed Major 7th
(Cont'd)

Ever wonder what to play on a major 7th with a ♯5? Now you have a phrase. This idea came from using a melodic minor scale down a minor 3rd from the chord.

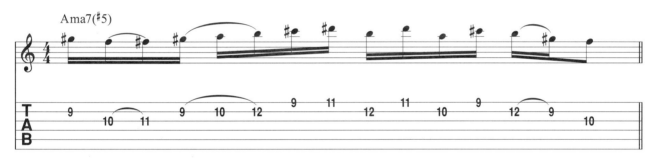

95   X • tend • ing Scale Shapes #1

This line begins with a "shape" from a second-position C scale and walks vertically up the neck. Notice how the idea keeps a similar contour as it moves.

X • tend • ing Scale Shapes #2

This phrase literally takes one shape and maintains it as it walks down the neck. All the notes, however, still remain diatonic.

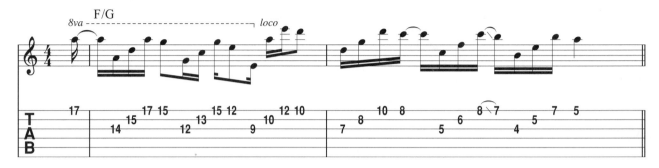

X • tend • ing Scale Shapes #3

This Lydian line has a nice open feel, starting off with some extended major 9ths. Pay careful at-tention to the slides in this one.

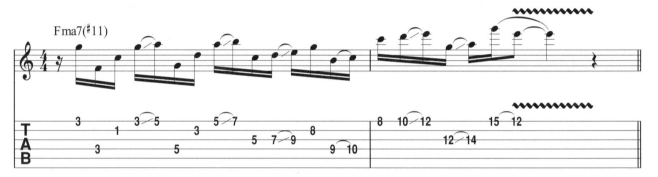

96 Yard • birds

This neat lick can be found on an old Yardbirds record. Jeff Beck has a way of coming up with extremely cool pull-off licks. Here he takes a seventh-position box pattern and incorporates an open B string for a great intervallic jumping idea. There is a pull-off from the E on the seventh fret, but the open G is used more as a dead note. When you hit the low D on the fifth fret, give it a little bend to add some attitude.

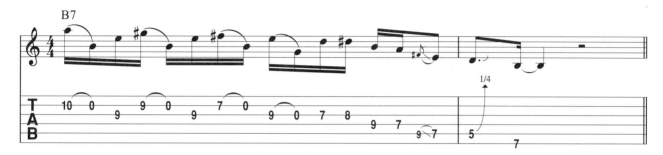

97 Y • 2 • K Rock

This modern rock lick is definitely ready for the new century. It starts off with a wide-open sound using 5th intervals and combines slides and finger stretches to move up the neck. To negotiate position shifts, pay attention to the tablature. This concept of moving through positions with slides has a lot of potential. Try making up some lines of your own in this style.

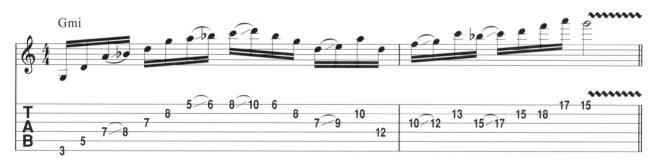

Z

98 Zone Doub • les

Here's a neat lick that utilizes doubled notes. It fits in the typical box position, but the fingering is important to get the right feel. Alternating the G between the second and third strings creates the effect. Pay attention to the tab and pull-offs. After you get the left hand synced with the right, you can pick up the tempo and really start to shred!

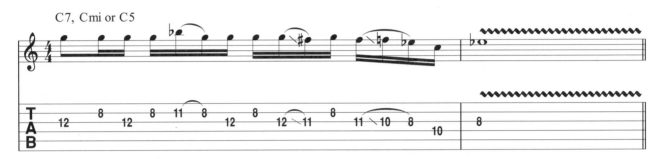

99 Z • Z Top

Are there any guys with long beards who rock harder than ZZ Top? I doubt it… Here's one of their classic riffs. Play it lightly, then build it to a heavy shuffle with distortion.

GUITAR NOTATION LEGEND

Guitar Music can be notated three different ways: on a *musical staff*, in *tablature*, and in *rhythm slashes*.

RHYTHM SLASHES are written above the staff. Strum chords in the rhythm indicated. Use the chord diagrams found at the top of the first page of the transcription for the appropriate chord voicings. Round noteheads indicate single notes.

THE MUSICAL STAFF shows pitches and rhythms and is divided by bar lines into measures. Pitches are named after the first seven letters of the alphabet.

TABLATURE graphically represents the guitar fingerboard. Each horizontal line represents a string, and each number represents a fret.

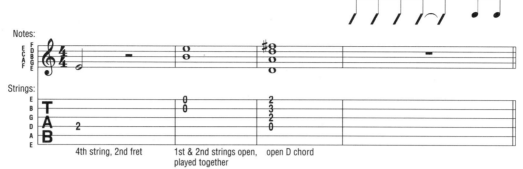

4th string, 2nd fret   1st & 2nd strings open, open D chord
played together

HALF-STEP BEND: Strike the note and bend up 1/2 step.

WHOLE-STEP BEND: Strike the note and bend up one step.

GRACE NOTE BEND: Strike the note and bend up as indicated. The first note does not take up any time.

SLIGHT (MICROTONE) BEND: Strike the note and bend up 1/4 step.

BEND AND RELEASE: Strike the note and bend up as indicated, then release back to the original note. Only the first note is struck.

PRE-BEND: Bend the note as indicated, then strike it.

VIBRATO: The string is vibrated by rapidly bending and releasing the note with the fretting hand.

WIDE VIBRATO: The pitch is varied to a greater degree by vibrating with the fretting hand.

HAMMER-ON: Strike the first (lower) note with one finger, then sound the higher note (on the same string) with another finger by fretting it without picking.

PULL-OFF: Place both fingers on the notes to be sounded. Strike the first note and without picking, pull the finger off to sound the second (lower) note.

LEGATO SLIDE: Strike the first note and then slide the same fret-hand finger up or down to the second note. The second note is not struck.

SHIFT SLIDE: Same as legato slide, except the second note is struck.

TRILL: Very rapidly alternate between the notes indicated by continuously hammering on and pulling off.

TAPPING: Hammer ("tap") the fret indicated with the pick-hand index or middle finger and pull off to the note fretted by the fret hand.

NATURAL HARMONIC: Strike the note while the fret-hand lightly touches the string directly over the fret indicated.

PINCH HARMONIC: The note is fretted normally and a harmonic is produced by adding the edge of the thumb or the tip of the index finger of the pick hand to the normal pick attack.

PICK SCRAPE: The edge of the pick is rubbed down (or up) the string, producing a scratchy sound.

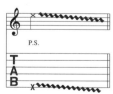

MUFFLED STRINGS: A percussive sound is produced by laying the fret hand across the string(s) without depressing, and striking them with the pick hand.

PALM MUTING: The note is partially muted by the pick hand lightly touching the string(s) just before the bridge.

RAKE: Drag the pick across the strings indicated with a single motion.

TREMOLO PICKING: The note is picked as rapidly and continuously as possible.

VIBRATO BAR DIVE AND RETURN: The pitch of the note or chord is dropped a specified number of steps (in rhythm) then returned to the original pitch.

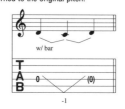

VIBRATO BAR SCOOP: Depress the bar just before striking the note, then quickly release the bar.

VIBRATO BAR DIP: Strike the note and then immediately drop a specified number of steps, then release back to the original pitch.

Musicians Institute Press

is the official series of Southern California's renowned music school, Musicians Institute. **MI** instructors, some of the finest musicians in the world, share their vast knowledge and experience with you – no matter what your current level. For guitar, bass, drums, vocals, and keyboards, **MI Press** offers the finest music curriculum for higher learning through a variety of series:

ESSENTIAL CONCEPTS
Designed from MI core curriculum programs.

MASTER CLASS
Designed from MI elective courses.

PRIVATE LESSONS
Tackle a variety of topics "one-on-one" with MI faculty instructors.

BASS

Arpeggios for Bass
by Dave Keif • Private Lessons
00695133 .... $12.95

The Art of Walking Bass
A Method for Acoustic or Electric Bass
by Bob Magnusson • Master Class
00695168 Book/CD Pack $17.95

Bass Fretboard Basics
by Paul Farnen • Essential Concepts
00695201 .... $12.95

Bass Playing Techniques
by Alexis Sklarevski • Essential Concepts
00695207 .... $16.95

Grooves for Electric Bass
by David Keif • Private Lessons
00695265 Book/CD Pack $14.95

Latin Bass
The Essential Guide to Afro-Cuban and Brazilian Styles
by George Lopez and David Keif • Private Lessons
00695543 Book/CD Pack $14.95

Music Reading for Bass
by Wendy Wrehovcsik • Essential Concepts
00695203 .... $9.95

Odd-Meter Bassics
by Dino Monoxelos • Private Lessons
00695170 Book/CD Pack $14.95

GUITAR

Advanced Scale Concepts & Licks for Guitar
by Jean Marc Belkadi • Private Lessons
00695298 Book/CD Pack $14.95

Basic Blues Guitar
by Steve Trovato • Private Lessons
00695180 Book/CD Pack $12.95

Contemporary Acoustic Guitar
by Eric Paschal & Steve Trovato • Master Class
00695320 Book/CD Pack $14.95

Classical & Fingerstyle Guitar Techniques
by David Oakes • Master Class
00695171 Book/CD Pack $14.95

Creative Chord Shapes
by Jamie Findlay • Private Lessons
00695172 Book/CD Pack $9.95

Diminished Scale for Guitar
by Jean Marc Belkadi • Private Lessons
00695227 Book/CD Pack $9.95

Essential Rhythm Guitar
Patterns, Progressions and Techniques for All Styles
by Steve Trovato • Private Lessons
00695181 Book/CD Pack $14.95

Funk Guitar: The Essential Guide
by Ross Bolton • Private Lessons
00695419 Book/CD Pack $9.95

Guitar Basics
by Bruce Buckingham • Private Lessons
00695134 Book/CD Pack $14.95

Guitar Hanon
by Peter Deneff • Private Lessons
00695321 .... $9.95

Guitar Soloing
by Dan Gilbert & Beth Marlis • Essential Concepts
00695190 Book/CD Pack.................... $19.95

Harmonics for Guitar
by Jamie Findlay • Private Lessons
00695169 Book/CD Pack $9.95

Jazz Guitar Chord System
by Scott Henderson • Private Lessons
00695291 .... $6.95

Jazz Guitar Improvisation
by Sid Jacobs • Master Class
00695128 Book/CD Pack $17.95

Jazz-Rock Triad Improvising
by Jean Marc Belkadi • Private Lessons
00695361 Book/CD Pack $12.95

Latin Guitar
The Essential Guide to Brazilian and Afro-Cuban Rhythms
by Bruce Buckingham • Master Class
00695379 Book/CD Pack $14.95

Modern Approach to Jazz, Rock & Fusion Guitar
by Jean Marc Belkadi • Private Lessons
00695143 Book/CD Pack $14.95

Modes for Guitar
by Tom Kolb • Private Lessons
00695555 Book/CD Pack $16.95

Music Reading for Guitar
by David Oakes • Essential Concepts
00695192 .... $16.95

The Musician's Guide to Recording Acoustic Guitar
by Dallan Beck • Private Lessons
00695505 Book/CD Pack $12.95

Practice Trax for Guitar
by Danny Gill • Private Lessons
00695601 Book/CD Pack $14.95

Rhythm Guitar
by Bruce Buckingham & Eric Paschal • Essential Concepts
00695188 .... $16.95

Rock Lead Basics
by Nick Nolan & Danny Gill • Master Class
00695144 Book/CD Pack $14.95

Rock Lead Performance
by Nick Nolan & Danny Gill • Master Class
00695278 Book/CD Pack $16.95

Rock Lead Techniques
by Nick Nolan & Danny Gill • Master Class
00695146 Book/CD Pack $14.95

Texas Blues Guitar
by Robert Calva • Private Lessons
00695340 Book/CD Pack $14.95

KEYBOARD

Funk Keyboards – The Complete Method
A Contemporary Guide to Chords, Rhythms, and Licks
by Gail Johnson • Master Class
00695336 Book/CD Pack $14.95

Jazz Hanon
by Peter Deneff • Private Lessons
00695554 .... $12.95

Keyboard Technique
by Steve Weingard • Essential Concepts
00695365 .... $12.95

Keyboard Voicings: The Complete Guide
by Kevin King • Essential Concepts
00695209 .... $12.95

Music Reading for Keyboard
by Larry Steelman • Essential Concepts
00695205 .... $12.95

R&B Soul Keyboards
by Henry J. Brewer • Private Lessons
00695327 Book/CD Pack $16.95

Salsa Hanon
by Peter Deneff • Private Lessons
00695226 .... $10.95

DRUM

Afro-Cuban Coordination for Drumset
by Maria Martinez • Private Lessons
00695328 Book/CD Pack $14.95

Brazilian Coordination for Drumset
by Maria Martinez • Master Class
00695284 Book/CD Pack $14.95

Chart Reading Workbook for Drummers
by Bobby Gabriele • Private Lessons
00695129 Book/CD Pack $14.95

Drummer's Guide to Odd Meters
by Ed Roscehi • Essential Concepts
00695349 Book/CD Pack $14.95

Latin Soloing for Drumset
by Phil Maturano • Private Lessons
00695287 Book/CD Pack.................... $14.95

Working the Inner Clock for Drumset
by Phil Maturano • Private Lessons
00695127 Book/CD Pack.................... $16.95

VOICE

Harmony Vocals: The Essential Guide
by Mike Campbell & Tracee Lewis • Private Lessons
00695262 Book/CD Pack.................... $16.95

Sightsinging
by Mike Campbell • Essential Concepts
00695195 .... $16.95

ALL INSTRUMENTS

An Approach to Jazz Improvisation
by Dave Pozzi • Private Lessons
00695135 Book/CD Pack $17.95

Encyclopedia of Reading Rhythms
by Gary Hess • Private Lessons
00695145 .... $19.95

Going Pro
by Kenny Kerner • Private Lessons
00695322 .... $16.95

Harmony & Theory
by Keith Wyatt & Carl Schroeder • Essential Concepts
00695161 .... $17.95

Lead Sheet Bible
by Robin Randall • Private Lessons
00695130 Book/CD Pack $19.95

WORKSHOP SERIES

Transcribed scores of the greatest songs ever!

Blues Workshop
00695137 .... $22.95

Classic Rock Workshop
00695136 .... $19.95

FOR MORE INFORMATION, SEE YOUR LOCAL MUSIC DEALER,
OR WRITE TO:

HAL•LEONARD®
CORPORATION
7777 W. BLUEMOUND RD. P.O. BOX 13819 MILWAUKEE, WI 53213
Visit Hal Leonard Online at
www.halleonard.com

Prices, contents, and availability subject to change without notice. Some products may not be available outside of the U.S.A.

0801